W9-BPP-081

THE LOGIC OF PREFERENCE

GEORG HENRIK VON WRIGHT

THE LOGIC OF PREFERENCE

An Essay

AT THE UNIVERSITY PRESS

EDINBURGH

EDINBURGH UNIVERSITY PRESS
22 George Square, Edinburgh
ISBN 0 85224 121 6
North America
Aldine Publishing Company
529 South Wabash Avenue, Chicago
Printed in Great Britain by
T & A Constable Ltd, Edinburgh
Reprinted 1971

PREFACE

This essay is an expanded version of one of a series of four lectures which I had the honour of giving in the University of Edinburgh in May 1962, under the auspices of the Northern Scholars Committee. The series was called 'Ethics and Logic'. I wish to express my thanks to the University for having invited me to lecture and to the University Press for its readiness to publish, in book form, my paper on the Logic of Preference.

The concept of preference which, from a formal logical point of view, is studied in this essay is, roughly speaking, the same as the notion of *liking* one thing *better* (more) than another. It is, moreover, a notion of intrinsic or sheer liking—of preferring something for its own sake or in itself to something else. It could also be called a notion of pure preference.

I think that this concept of preference is of pivotal importance to theory of value in general and to its three principal branches—aesthetics, economics, and ethics. Its function seems to me to be that of a kind of 'value-radical' or common root of aesthetic, economic, and moral valuations. This is not, of course, to say that all such valuations could be 'reduced' to pure preferences; but it is to maintain that a full analysis of value-concepts in aesthetics, economics, and ethics will reveal that the notion of a pure preference is a conceptual ingredient which many, if not all, those concepts have in common. An understanding of the nature of pure preferences is therefore not only helpful but moreover essential to a better understanding of the more complex forms of valuation.

November, 1962 GEORG HENRIK VON WRIGHT

THE LOGIC OF PREFERENCE

§ 1

The concepts in which moral philosophers take an interest may be divided into three groups. Concepts of the first group I shall call *deontological* or *normative*. Prominent among them are the notions of right and duty, command, permission, and prohibition. Concepts of the second group I shall call *axiological* or *value-concepts*. Prominent among them, in ethics, are the ideas of good and evil, and the comparative notion of betterness. Concepts of the third group I propose to call *anthropological*. To this belong, among others, the notions of need and want, decision and choice, motive, end and action.

The general study of the concepts of the first group can be called Deontology or General Theory of Norms; of the second group, Axiology or General Theory of Value. The general study of concepts of the third group could aptly be called Philosophical Anthropology. Ethics, or moral philosophy, is a special study of concepts of all three groups.

There are no sharp lines of division between the groups of concepts. It would be a mistake to think that the concepts of any one of the three groups could be successfully studied in relative isolation from those of the other groups. In particular, it is worth pointing out that the study of normative and value-concepts must be based on a more thorough examination than has traditionally been considered necessary, of concepts of the kind which I have called 'anthropological'. The basis of ethics or philosophy of morals must be an anthropology or philosophy of man.

The concepts of all three groups can be studied from several points of view. One is the formal logical point of view. It has long been neglected. One reason for this has been that until recently logic was itself a neglected province of philosophy. Another reason has been the prominence of the opinion, not least among contemporary philosophers, that norms and values are by nature 'alogical' and therefore not amenable to treatment by the methods of formal logic. This opinion is, I think, basically unsound. It has its root in misleading analogies and false identifications. It is a mistake to think of the distinction between 'logical' and 'alogical' as a parallel to the distinction between 'theoretical' and 'practical', in a philosophic sense. And it would also be a mistake to identify the province of logic with that of descriptive discourse and theoretical concept-structures.

In recent years there has been a growing interest in the logical study of norms. This study has to some extent been given a systematic form and become known under the name of Deontic Logic. I would not maintain that 'deontic logic' is an uncontroversial pursuit. I am, moreover, convinced that in all its presently-known forms it suffers from grave insufficiencies and, it may be, from errors. But it is also a fact that this young branch of the science of logic *exists*—and I do not think that future criticisms and corrections will be able to obliterate its very existence.

It is therefore tempting to consider whether there could be created, for the axiological notions, a counterpart to deontic logic. Logicians and philosophers have not been much concerned with this task. Few convincing or promising achievements can as yet be noted among the attempts which have been made to construct such a logic.

In the present essay I shall outline a formal system of a basic and (logically) rather 'primitive' type of valuations. I call them *preferences*. I shall also make a few—not very systematic—comments on questions of the logic of value generally.

§ 2

It seems to be a characteristic difference between normative notions and value-concepts that the former do not admit of *degrees*, but that the latter do so admit. The comparative notions of better and worse are as familiar and important as the absolute notions of good and bad. But it is problematic whether there exist comparative notions of obligation and prohibition. One sometimes says that one act is more urgently obligatory than another, or more strictly prohibited. But such locutions are not very common. And one hardly ever uses the phrases 'more obligatory' or 'more prohibited' without an adverb such as 'urgently' or 'strongly' or 'strictly', between the words.

The words 'better' and 'worse' can be understood to denote that which logicians call *converses* of each other. When understood in this way, to say that x is better than y is to say that y is worse than x, and *vice versa*. The two notions are inter-definable. One can, in a sense, regard them as *one* concept.[1]

It seems to be generally true that value-concepts form *triples* of two value-absolutes ('at each end') and one value-comparative ('between them'). 'Good', 'bad', and 'better' are not the only example. 'Beautiful', 'ugly', and 'more (less) beautiful (ugly)' are another.

A problem of primary interest to a logical study of values is the mutual relationship of the members of such triples of concepts. Is it, for example, possible to define the two absolutes of a triple in terms of one another—as it is obviously possible to define obligation and prohibition in terms of one another with the aid of negation and the distinction between doing and forbearing? Or can the absolutes be defined in terms of the comparative, or the comparative in terms of the absolutes?

These questions have been relatively little investigated. It would be tempting to think that they could be answered in the same way for *all* triples of value-concepts. But there seem to be reasons

[1] Although the words 'better' and 'worse' can be and sometimes are used to denote a relation and its converse, they are not always so used. 'Better' sometimes means the same as 'good in a higher degree', and 'worse' sometimes means 'bad in a higher degree'. Then the converse of betterness is called 'less good', and the converse of being worse is called 'less bad'. On this second use of 'better' and 'worse' it is incorrect to say of two (unequally) good things that the one is worse than the other. Similarly, it would be incorrect to say of two bad things that the one is better than the other.

against assuming that they can be thus uniformly answered.

There are several forms or varieties of goodness —and correspondingly of badness and betterness. Instead of speaking of forms of goodness, we could also speak of several senses or uses of the word 'good'. The triple 'good-bad-better' is thus not, it appears, *one* triple of concepts. There are several triples of the same name. It cannot be taken for granted that all triples, which fall under the name 'good-bad-better', conform to the same logical pattern as far as the relations of their members to one another are concerned.

I am not aware of any successful attempt (or promising possibility) at defining goodness and badness in terms of each other (without relying on the comparative notion), or of defining betterness in terms of the absolute notions. But I shall try to show in this essay that there is at least *one* pair of notions 'good' and 'bad' which can be defined in terms of a notion of 'better'.

§ 3

I shall not, however, make the notion of betterness the starting-point of my inquiry. As indicated on p. 9, the point of departure will be the notion of *preference*.

There are several types of preference, and several grounds on which one may distinguish between them. One means of distinguishing is the general character of the things, between which a relation of preference holds. Here I shall mention three types:

(*a*) Sometimes (the use of) one instrument is preferred to (the use of) another instrument, for a certain purpose. For example: This knife is preferred to that knife for cutting meat.

(*b*) Sometimes one way of doing a thing is preferred to another way of doing the same thing. For example: We may prefer to travel to a certain destination by train rather than by bus.

(*c*) Sometimes one state of affairs is preferred to another state of affairs. Normal people normally prefer health to illness. Some people may prefer to have an occupation with a lower salary and more time for leisure, to an occupation with higher pay but heavier work and more responsibility. Others have the opposite preference.

This list of types of preference according to types of things, between which there is a preference-relation, is not meant to be exhaustive. Nor is it maintained that the types mentioned are logically independent. It may be suggested that, of the three types, preferences between states hold a basic position, and that the two other types may become somehow 'reduced' or 'translated' into it. I shall not here examine the plausibility of this suggestion. But I shall explicitly limit the formal theory, which we are going to construct, to preferences between *states of affairs*.

§ 4

A preference, of any type, is necessarily relative to a subject. A preference is always *somebody's* preference. When speaking of an unspecified subject, however, it is sometimes convenient to use the impersonal mode of speech: 'is preferred', instead of the personal: 'so and so prefers'.

A preference, moreover, is relative, not only to a subject but also to a certain moment or occasion or station in the life of a subject. Not only may different people have different preferences, but one and the same man may revise his preferences in the course of his life. Perhaps, when he was young, he preferred on his holidays to go hunting rather than yachting, but in his middle age preferred to go on a yachting-trip to going on a hunting-expedition.

§ 5

The concept of preference is related to the notion of betterness. It is also related to the notion of choice. Betterness is a typically axiological notion. Choice belongs, again, to the group of concepts which I have called anthropological. Because of its double relationship, to betterness and to choice, the concept of preference itself may be said to stand between the two groups of concepts.

How is preference related to betterness?

There appear to be forms of betterness (forms of 'the good') which stand in no immediate, intrinsic relationship to preference at all. I am thinking in particular of a form of goodness which could be called *technical*. I mean goodness of skill (ability, talent). What has the fact that *x* is a better chess player or a better painter than *y* to do with preference? So far as I can see, there is no immediate connexion. But there may exist remote connexions. Sometimes, for example, technical goodness has a connexion with *instrumental* goodness, *i.e.* goodness for a purpose. If *x* is a better doctor than *y*, we may prefer to consult *x* rather than *y* when we are anxious to become cured of some serious illness. This case is like preferring a sharp knife to a blunt one when we want to sharpen a pencil.

All forms of preference appear to stand in an intrinsic relationship to goodness. But this intrinsic relation can be of (at least) two different kinds:

Sometimes a certain thing is preferred to another thing, *because* the former is known or thought to be better (in a certain regard) than the latter. A person says, for example, that he prefers claret to hock, because his doctor has told him or he has found from experience that the first wine is better for his stomach or health generally. In this case a *judgment of betterness* serves as a *ground* or *reason* for a preference. I shall call preferences, which hold this relationship to betterness, *extrinsic.*

It could, however, also be the case that a person prefers claret to hock, not because he thinks (opines) that the first wine is better for him, but simply because he likes the first better (more). Then his liking the one wine better is not a reason for his preference. It is therefore not, strictly speaking, correct to say that he prefers the one *because* he likes it better than the other. That he likes the one wine better and that he prefers it to the other wine amount to the same thing. But he may *choose* ('prefer to choose') the one, because he likes it better than (= prefers it to) the other. I shall say that preference in this case is *constitutive* of betterness. And I shall call preferences, which hold this relation to betterness, *intrinsic*.

It is with intrinsic preferences, and with them alone, that the formal theory, which will be developed presently, is concerned. Intrinsic preference, one could also say, is a *form of betterness*. The meaning of my somewhat technical phrase 'intrinsically to prefer' is *roughly* the same as what, in ordinary language, we mean by 'to like better (more)'. An (intrinsic) preference, one could say with the *Oxford Dictionary*, is the 'liking of one thing more than another'.

§ 6

Choice based on preference is called *preferential choice*. How is intrinsic preference related to preferential choice?

It is obvious that there can exist intrinsic preferences, even when there is no question of *actually* choosing between things. A person can significantly be said to prefer a mild rainy day to hot sunshine, even though he cannot choose between the two states. We all normally prefer health to illness. But only under exceptional circumstances, if ever, can a man be significantly said to choose to be well or ill. Nor do we choose the weather.

The question may be raised, however, whether

a preference ought not to entail a *potential* choice between things or states. A person, it could be argued, who prefers mild weather to hot sunshine *would* go to a place where it is mild, rather than to one where the sun is shining hot, *if* he had a choice and *if* no other preferences of his were affected by his option.

I wish to stress that it would be wrong to identify preference with preferential choice, and that what we are studying here are preferences, and not preferential choices or options.

§ 7

The notion of preference, as is well known, holds a prominent place in economic theory. The formal study of preference and of value generally is prominent in economics and in the related fields known as econometrics and decision theory. Before we proceed to construct a formal logic of preferences, some few remarks should be made on the economist's notion of preference.

In economic theory preferences are usually studied in close connexion with the notions of *utility* and *probability*. The relations between the three concepts are themselves a problem of major interest. According to a view which has found favour with many recent authors, one can employ a notion of preference for defining a notion of equal (subjective) probability. These notions of preference and equi-probability can then be used for defining a (metric) notion of utility. In terms of preference and utility, finally, one can define a notion of an arbitrary degree of probability.[1]

I shall not in this essay discuss utility, or 'measurable value', at all. Nor shall I discuss probability. I mention the two chiefly for the following reason:

It is plausible to think that neither utility nor subjective probability can be defined independently of preferences. Whether utility can be defined independently of probability and probability independently of utility is debatable. But that preferences, at least of some basic kind, can be studied independently of questions of utility and probability seems highly plausible. Nevertheless, this independent study, to the best of my knowledge, has never been systematically undertaken *from a formal logical point of view.* Authors on these topics usually take for granted certain logical features of preferences—such as asymmetry and transitivity—and then hasten on to utility (and/or probability). They tend, as it were, to shift as quickly as possible from 'qualitative' considerations of a 'logical' nature to 'quantitative' con-

[1] This view of the interconnectedness of preference, utility, and subjective probability seems to have been first suggested by F. P. Ramsay in his ingenious essay 'Truth and Probability', published posthumously in *Foundations of Mathematics and other Logical Essays* (London 1931). Substantially the same view is adopted by Davidson, McKinsey, and Suppes in their important paper 'Outlines of a Formal Theory of Value' in *Philosophy of Science*, vol. *22*, 1955. For a brief restatement of the view with some critical comments on it the reader may be referred to my paper 'Remarks on the Epistemology of Subjective Probability' in *Logic, Methodology and Philosophy of Science*, Proceedings of the 1960 International Congress (Stanford 1962).

siderations of a 'mathematical' nature. The temptation to do so may be understandable. Yet I think it is worth resisting for the sake of first creating a systematic formal theory of ('pure') preferences: not least when we consider the basic position which preference holds in relation to utility, a Logic of Preference may be regarded as an urgent *desideratum* of an up-to-date utility theory.

The only attempt on somewhat similar lines to mine, so far as I am aware, is by Sören Halldén in his book *On the Logic of 'Better'*.[1] It deserves, in my opinion, much credit as a pioneer work. The notion of betterness, with which the author deals, is a relation between states. In this important feature it resembles the notion of preference, the subject of our attempt to construct a formal theory. Many of Halldén's results are valid within the present formalism. But there are also important differences in basic principles between the two theories.

§ 8

Arbitrary states of affairs will be symbolized by lower-case letters p, q, r, . . . We shall regard the letters as schematic representations of sentences, which describe generic states of affairs.

By calling the states *generic* I mean that they may or may not obtain on any given occasion and that they can obtain on more than one occasion. To be well and to be ill are generic states; a man is now well and now ill, and he can be ill on many occasions (many times) in the course of his life.

[1] Library of Theoria, No. 2, Uppsala, 1957.

Of the variables p, q, r, . . . molecular compounds may be constructed by means of truth-connectives. I shall use '$\sim$' as a symbol for negation, '&' for conjunction, 'v' for disjunction, '$\rightarrow$' for (material) implication, and '$\leftrightarrow$' for (material) equivalence.

I shall assume that my readers are familiar with the elementary branch of formal logic called the Logic of Propositions (the Propositional Calculus, sometimes also called the Sentential Calculus). Two important and useful techniques of this elementary theory are the construction of truth-tables and the transformation of expressions into various so-called *normal* forms.

As a symbol for the preference-relation I shall use the capital letter P. An expression, which consists of the letter P with a variable, or a molecular compound of variables, to its left and to its right, I shall call an *atomic* P-expression or preference-expression.

Thus, for example, pPq and $(p\&q)P\sim r$ are atomic P-expressions. The first can be read: (the state) p is preferred to (the state) q. The second can be read: (the state) p *and* q is preferred to (the state) not-r.

Preferences, it should be remembered, are relative to a subject and an occasion (station, time). Thus pPq, for example, symbolizes an unspecified subject's preference of the state p to the state q on some unspecified occasion. I shall say, moreover, that pPq symbolizes a *generic* preference. If a preference of the kind in question happens to be an individual subject's preference on some specific occasion, we speak of an *individual* preference.

Atomic P-expressions can be combined with molecular compounds by means of truth-connectives. Atomic P-expressions and their molecular compounds will be called *P-expressions* or *preference-expressions*.[1]

For example: $\sim(pPq)\rightarrow(p\&q)P\sim r$ is a (molecular) P-expression. It can be read: If it is not the case that p is preferred to q, then it is the case that p *and*

[1] I shall adopt the following conventions for the use of quotation-marks round symbolic expressions:

In phrases such as *the sign P*, or *the variable p*, or *the expression pPq* no quotes will be used. Similarly, in phrases such as *the state p* or *the preference pPq*. When no qualifying attribute such as 'sign' or 'state' is being used to indicate, whether we are talking about the symbols or about the things symbolized, we shall use quotes, when the context mentions the *symbol*, and no quotes when the context mentions the thing symbolized. For example: ≫'p' in 'pPq' stands to the left of 'P'≫ speaks about symbols. 'The subject prefers $p\&q$ to $\sim r$' speaks about things (states) symbolized by certain symbols.

The conventions, which we adopt for the use of brackets should be obvious to the reader from the contexts. Let it, however, be explicitly stated that the conjunction-sign has a stronger binding force than the disjunction-sign. Thus, for example, the formula $p\&q\vee p\&r$ should be read as a two-termed disjunction of two-termed conjunctions—and *not* as a three-termed conjunction, one term of which is a disjunction. This second formula is written $p\&(q\vee p)\&r$.

The terms 'negation', 'conjunction', 'disjunction' and a few others are used in such a way that they apply both to symbols and to the things symbolized. Thus, *e.g.*, we shall speak both of the conjunction of two or more expressions and of the conjunction of two or more states. The first conjunction is a (compound) expression. The second is a (compound) state.

I shall often say of *expressions* that they are consistent or inconsistent and say that an expression entails another or is a tautology or a truth-function of other expressions. Primarily, these properties (consistency, *etc.*) of the expressions, are features of the *propositions* expressed by those expressions.

q is preferred to not-*r*. It is important to remember that the *entire* *P*-expression must be taken relative to a subject and an occasion. It symbolizes one and the same unspecified subject's preference on one and the same unspecified occasion.

The formal study and theory of *P*-expressions I shall call the (basic) Logic of Preference. As an alternative name I would suggest Prohairetic Logic—from the Greek word for preference (and preferential choice) προαίρεσις.

§ 9

The Logic of Preference which I propose to construct rests on five basic principles. We could perhaps call them 'axioms'. I shall not, however, present the system in the form of an axiomatic calculus. I shall present it in the form of a *technique* for deciding whether any given *P*-expression does or does not express a proposition which is logically true.

The five basic principles fall into two groups. The first group has two, the second three members. The two principles which belong to the first group may be said to concern the formal properties of the *relation* of preference. Use of the three principles of the second group makes it possible to transform any given *P*-expression into a standard form, to which the decision-technique can then be applied.

The formal properties of the relation of preference are *asymmetry* and *transitivity*.

Asymmetry means that, if one state is preferred to another, then necessarily the second state is not preferred to the first: that is, by the same subject on the same occasion. This seems perfectly clear and uncontroversial.

Transitivity means that, if one state is preferred to another and this second is preferred to a third, then necessarily the first state too is preferred to the third state.

The transitivity of the relation of preference is not entirely uncontroversial. It is possible to imagine situations which may appear to be counter-instances to the transitivity of preferences.

Suppose a person is offered, 'on a tray', a choice between an orange and a banana. He chooses the orange. He is then offered a choice between a banana and an apple. He chooses the banana. Finally he has to face a choice between an orange and an apple. Is he then 'by the laws of logic' bound to choose the orange? Does he 'contradict' himself, in thought or action, if he chooses the apple?

It is *not* obvious how we should answer these questions. Note that the case was described in terms of *choices* on *successive occasions* for choosing. The choices are evidently preferential choices. But whether we shall think of the preferences 'behind' the choices as *extrinsic* or *intrinsic* is left open in the description.

If the subject made his third choice contrary to transitivity, then we should, I think, have to react to the case in one of two ways. Either we should have to say that the subject has *changed* his preferences in the course of the succession of occasions. Or we should have to look for *reasons* for his choices, to ask him *why* he preferred an orange to a banana, *why* he preferred a banana to an apple, and *why*—in spite of these preferences—he now prefers an apple to an orange. Maybe reasons can be given which would remove the impression of a contradiction or an incompatibility. (I am uncertain about this.) Then, however, the subject's preferences would have been of the sort which I have called *extrinsic* (cf. p. 14). If the subject insisted on the *intrinsic* nature of his preferences (said they were 'sheer likings'), our reaction would be, I think, that he must either have changed his preferences—or else that we do not understand him.

The preferences which we shall study are a subject's intrinsic preferences on one occasion only. Thus we exclude both *reasons* for preferences and the possibility of *changes* in preferences.

Is it logically possible that a subject on some occasion could intrinsically prefer a first state to a second and this second to a third, and yet prefer the third state to the first? It seems to me that, however interesting and realistic various examples of non-transitivity may be, they could not support an affirmative answer to *this* question. I shall therefore assume that the relation of preference, which we are here studying, is transitive.

§ 10

Let us ask: What *is* it (what does it *mean*) to prefer one state of affairs to another? We cannot, here, consider all aspects of this complex and difficult question. But we shall comment on some aspects which are relevant to our formal theory of preferences.

The first comment concerns a connexion between *preference* and *change*.

Consider two generic states p and q. At any given moment (on any given occasion) both states might obtain, or one of them, or neither. The world, one could also say, must necessarily be a $p\&q$-world or a $p\&\sim q$-world or a $\sim p\&q$-world or a $\sim p\&\sim q$-world.

A subject says he prefers p to q. It is useful to consider the meaning of this valuation in relation to the four possible ways in which the subject's present world may be constituted with regard to the two generic states p and q.

Assume that p and q both obtain. The subject already 'has' both p and q 'in his world'. That he prefers p to q must then mean that he would rather lose q (and retain p) than lose p (and retain q). He would, in other words, rather see his present situation changed from $p\&q$ to $p\&\sim q$ than see it changed from $p\&q$ to $\sim p\&q$.

Assume that $p\&\sim q$ is the case. To prefer p to q in a world, where p is and q is not, must mean that one would rather see this world remain the same than see it changed into a $\sim p\&q$-world. One would, in other words, rather retain p and continue to be without q than lose p and get q 'in compensation'.

Assume that $\sim p\&q$ is the case. Then to prefer p to q must mean to prefer that the world should change from $\sim p$ to p and from q to $\sim q$ rather than that it should remain unchanged in both its present features.

Assume, finally, that neither p nor q obtains. Then to prefer p to q must mean that one would rather get p and continue to be without q than get q and continue to be without p. The subject, in other words, would rather see his present world changed from $\sim p \& \sim q$ to $p \& \sim q$ than see it changed from $\sim p \& \sim q$ to $\sim p \& q$.

Thus, in all four cases, to say that a subject prefers p to q is tantamount to saying that he prefers $p \& \sim q$ to $\sim p \& q$ as *end-states of contemplated possible changes in his present situation* (whatever that be).[1]

§ II

Preferences between disjunctive states, or between a disjunction of states and a single state, raise special problems. What does it mean, for example, to prefer the state p *or* q to the state r?

On the basis of what was said in the last section, one step towards answering this question becomes immediately clear. To prefer $p \vee q$ to r is to prefer $(p \vee q) \& \sim r$ to $\sim p \& \sim q \& r$. $(p \vee q) \& \sim r$ again is the same state as $p \& q \& \sim r \vee p \& \sim q \& \sim r \vee \sim p \& q \& \sim r$. The preference of $p \vee q$ to r is thus the same as the preference of this three-termed disjunction of three-termed conjunctions of states to the one three-termed conjunction of states $\sim p \& \sim q \& r$.

The question which we have now to answer is whether and in what way this last preference is

[1] We then count the possibility that the world remains unchanged as one of the possible ways, in which it may become 'changed'. This is a useful terminological generalization.

'distributive'. It is helpful to consider this question in the light of an example:

A person says that he would prefer increased pay in his job *or* longer holidays to fewer working hours in the day. Let us assume that the two members of the disjunction are not exclusive of one another. Then his preference means that he would prefer a higher salary and longer holidays but no reduction of his amount of daily work *or* higher pay but neither longer holidays nor less work *or* longer holidays but neither higher pay nor less work to less work but neither higher pay nor longer holidays. 'Would prefer' here means roughly the same as 'would like better (welcome it more), if he got it'.

From the case, as we have described it, it may seem fairly obvious that the person's preference is tantamount to a conjunction of the following three preferences: He prefers higher pay and longer holidays to reduced working hours; he also prefers (only) higher pay to reduced working hours; and he prefers (only) longer holidays to reduced working hours.

Generally speaking: To prefer p *or* q to r is to prefer $p\&q\&\sim r$ to $\sim p\&\sim q\&r$ *and* prefer $p\&\sim q\&\sim r$ to $\sim p\&\sim q\&r$ *and* prefer $\sim p\&q\&\sim r$ to $\sim p\&\sim q\&r$. On the basis of analogical considerations one would reach the result that to prefer p to q *or* r is to prefer $p\&\sim q\&\sim r$ to $\sim p\&q\&r$ *and* prefer $p\&\sim q\&\sim r$ to $\sim p\&q\&\sim r$ *and* prefer $p\&\sim q\&\sim r$ to $\sim p\&\sim q\&r$. One could sum up these two distribution principles in the words: Disjunctive preferences are conjunctively distributive.

There is, however, an apparent counter-argument to the above distribution principle, which we must pause to consider.

Suppose an employer offers one of his employees the following *option*: The employee will be given a higher pay or longer holidays *or* his working hours will be reduced. He is not told, however, which of the two—higher pay or longer holidays—he will be given if he chooses the first alternative. He is then asked to make a choice.

Assume that our man would like most of all to get an increase in salary, but that he would prefer a reduction of his working hours to longer holidays. He might then, *e.g.* on the basis of his knowledge of his employer or of the nature of his job, argue as follows:

It is highly probable that, if I choose the first alternative, I shall get that which most of all I want, *viz.* an increase in my salary. It is possible, but rather unlikely, that I shall then get that which least of all I want (of the three things), *viz.* longer holidays. Therefore I take the risk (chance) and choose the first alternative. In view of the probabilities I consider this as the better (more advantageous) of the two.

We shall call a preference of this type a *preference involving risk.* A more adequate name would perhaps be preferential *choice* involving risk. Disjunctive preferences involving risk are not conjunctively distributive. For, in the above example, the subject preferred a disjunctive state of the form $p\&q\&\sim r v p\&\sim q\&\sim r v \sim p\&q\&\sim r$ to a state $\sim p\&\sim q\&r$ and yet also preferred $\sim p\&\sim q\&r$ to

$\sim p \& q \& \sim r$. This is not only consistent but can, under circumstances, be perfectly rational.

The person who is offered the above option might, however, also argue as follows:

Perhaps, if I choose the first alternative, I shall get that which most of all I want, *viz.* an increase in salary. But perhaps I shall then get that which least of all I want (of the three things), *viz.* only longer holidays. I have no idea which of the two possibilities is more likely to come true. I can take the risk and choose the first alternative. But I cannot consider the first alternative to be better (more advantageous) than the second, since I have no idea of the probabilities. As things stand (with regard to my knowledge and beliefs), I could consider the first alternative to be better, only if it were the case that, whatever I get if I choose it, I should get something which I value higher than that which I shall get if I choose the second.

Where a preference of a disjunction of states to a state (or of a state to a disjunction of states) is independent of the probabilities of the several members of the disjunction, then I shall call it a *preference not involving risk.*

Preferences which involve risk, and preferences which do not involve risk, are two types of preference. The two types obey different laws. Preferences without risk between disjunctive states are conjunctively distributive—preferences with risk are not. Our present study concerns preferences of the first type.

As far as I can see, the distinction between the two types of preference is connected with the distinction between preferential choice and ('pure') preference. Primarily, the things which involve risk here are *choices*. Our *likings*, as such, are independent of probabilities.

It seems to me, moreover, that the preferences, in terms of which subjective probabilities may become defined (cf. p. 16 f.), must be of the 'risk-free' type—or else the definition would involve a vicious circle. But I shall not argue the point here.

§ 12

The fifth and last basic principle of Prohairetic Logic, which remains to be explained, concerns something which I propose to call the *holistic* nature of preferences. It is perhaps their most peculiar feature, logically. Yet authors on these topics, as far as I can see, have habitually ignored it.

To prefer a state p to a state q, we said on p. 25, is to favour a change from the present state of the world, whatever it be, to a state $p \& \sim q$ over a change from the present state to $\sim p \& q$. Should this be understood to mean that we prefer the one change to the other, irrespective of how the world changes *in other features*, beside p and q? There are obviously several possibilities to be considered.

a] One possibility is that the subject actually welcomes a change to $p \& \sim q$ more than a change to $\sim p \& q$, irrespective of all other changes which may simultaneously happen to the world. If this is the case, I shall say that he prefers p to q *absolutely*.

Let r be some state which is different from p and q and which is not, in its turn, a truth-function of any other states. This state r either obtains or does not obtain in the world as it is at present. If a subject absolutely prefers p to q, then he will, irrespective of what his present situation is, welcome a change of it to a state $p\&\sim q\&r$ *or* $p\&\sim q\&\sim r$ more than a change of it to a state $\sim p\&q\&r$ *or* $\sim p\&q\&\sim r$. He will, in other words, prefer $p\&\sim q\&r$ to $\sim p\&q\&r$ and prefer $p\&\sim q\&r$ to $\sim p\&q\&\sim r$ and prefer $p\&\sim q\&\sim r$ to $\sim p\&q\&r$ and prefer $p\&\sim q\&\sim r$ to $\sim p\&q\&\sim r$. (This is in accordance with the principle of distribution, which we explained on p. 26.)

An absolute preference of p to q thus means that every total state of the world which contains p and $\sim q$ is preferred to every total state of the world which contains $\sim p$ and q.

The notion of absolute preference seems to be of comparatively little interest. This is probably due to the following logical peculiarity of absolute preferences:

A given subject can, at any given moment, have *at most one* absolute preference. This is easily shown by means of a *reductio ad absurdum* argument.

Assume that p were absolutely preferred to q and r absolutely preferred to s. From the first preference it follows that $p\&\sim q\&\sim r\&s$ is preferred to $\sim p\&q\&r\&\sim s$. From the second preference follows that $\sim p\&q\&r\&\sim s$ is preferred to $p\&\sim q\&\sim r\&s$. These conclusions contradict each other, since they conflict with the asymmetrical nature of the relation of preference. Hence, if p is absolutely preferred to q, r cannot be absolutely preferred to s, and *vice versa*.

b] Another possibility is that the subject favours a change to $p\&\sim q$ over a change to $\sim p\&q$, irrespective of what the state of the world *is*, but assuming that it does not *change* in other features beside p and q. If this is the case, I shall say that p is preferred to q *unconditionally*.

Let r be some state which is different from p and q and which is not, in its turn, a truth-function of any other states. This state r either obtains or does not obtain in the world, as it is at present. Assume that r is the case. Then, if a subject unconditionally prefers p to q, he would rather see the world change from its present state to a state $p\&\sim q\&r$ than see it change to a state $\sim p\&q\&r$. Assume that r is not the case. Then, if a subject unconditionally prefers p to q, he would rather see the world change from its present state to a state $p\&\sim q\&\sim r$ than see it change to a state $\sim p\&q\&\sim r$. On the first assumption, the subject prefers $p\&r$ to $q\&r$. (For, according to the explanation given on p. 24 f., to prefer $p\&r$ to $q\&r$ is to prefer $p\&r\&\sim(q\&r)$ to $q\&r\&\sim(p\&r)$—and $p\&r\&\sim(q\&r)$ is the same state as $p\&\sim q\&r$, and $q\&r\&\sim(p\&r)$ is the same state as $\sim p\&q\&r$.) On the second assumption again, the subject prefers $p\&\sim r$ to $q\&\sim r$.

An unconditional preference of p to q thus means that any given total state of the world, which contains p but not q, is preferred to a total state of the world, which differs from the first in that it contains q but not p, but otherwise is identical with it.

An unconditional preference is a preference

ceteris paribus. A person who unconditionally prefers, say, a raincoat to an umbrella, would, if he had both articles, rather lose his umbrella than his raincoat, assuming that he does not lose anything else which he has, nor get anything new which he has not. But he may unconditionally prefer a raincoat to an umbrella, and yet much prefer the loss of his raincoat alone to the loss of his umbrella *and* his shoes. And he may unconditionally prefer a raincoat to an umbrella, and yet prefer the loss of his raincoat to the loss of his umbrella, if he were given a sweater to protect him against the cold.

c] A third possibility is that the subject favours a change to $p\&\sim q$ over a change to $\sim p\&q$ on condition that the $p\&\sim q$-world and the $\sim p\&q$-world agree in a certain specified feature or features, but not otherwise. Then the subject has what I propose to call a *conditional* preference of p to q. If, in particular, the subject prefers $p\&\sim q\&r$ to $\sim p\&q\&r$, but does *not* prefer $p\&\sim q\&\sim r$ to $\sim p\&q\&\sim r$, I shall say that his preference of p to q is conditioned by r.

A person may, for example, prefer to lose his shirt to losing his shoes, provided he retains his trousers. But if in any case he has to lose his trousers, he may prefer to lose, in addition, his shoes rather than to lose, in addition, his shirt.

When, in this essay, I speak of preferences without qualifying them as 'absolute', 'unconditional', or 'conditional', what is meant are *unconditional preferences*. Our Logic of Preference thus is a logical theory of unconditional intrinsic preferences between states of affairs. It is in the *ceteris paribus* nature of the unconditional preferences that their 'holistic' character consists.

§ 13

The question may be raised: *Are there* unconditional preferences? For at least two reasons, it may be thought that the question has to be answered in the negative. The first reason is that the number of states of affairs, which may obtain at any given moment, is perhaps infinite and in any case is so great that no man can survey all the possible ways in which the states may be present or absent. How can he then ever be sure that a certain preference of his is invariant with regard to *all* combinations of accompanying circumstances—as has to be the case if the preference is unconditional? The second reason is that the notion of an unconditional preference, as we have defined it, seems to require that there are elementary states of affairs which are not themselves truth-functions of other states of affairs. But is not this assumption of 'simples' or of 'logical atomism' bad metaphysics?

One can, for the purposes of a formal calculus, evade the difficulties, which are raised by either question, by stipulating that the unconditionality of preferences shall be taken *relative to a given set of descriptions* of generic states of affairs. I shall call such a set a Universe of Discourse. An example would be the set of (schematic) sentences p, q, and r. That the state p is unconditionally preferred to the state q is to mean, within this Universe of Discourse, that the state $p\&r$ is preferred to the state $q\&r$ *and* the state $p\&\sim r$ to the state $q\&\sim r$.

We shall decide that the Universe of Discourse, (relative to which the preferences, described by the atomic constituents of a given preference-expression, are unconditional) is the set of *all* the variables p, q, r, . . . , which occur in the entire expression. This set we shall call the Universe of Discourse of the formula.

§ 14

In terms of the notion of an unconditional preference one can define a notion of goodness and of badness.

A state p is *good*, we shall say, if it is unconditionally preferred to its contradictory $\sim p$, *i.e.* if its presence is unconditionally preferred to its absence.

A state p is *bad*, we shall say, if its contradictory is unconditionally preferred to it, *i.e.* if its absence is unconditionally preferred to its presence.

These notions of goodness and badness, be it observed, are relative to a subject and to an occasion. What is good to one subject on some occasion may not be good to another subject on the same occasion or to the same subject on another occasion.

These notions of goodness and badness, also, are in a characteristic sense notions of *intrinsic* goodness and badness. 'Good/bad' here does *not* mean 'good/bad for some purpose' or 'good/bad for some being'. These are notions of *extrinsic* value. That something is good/bad to somebody shall be understood to mean that the subject judges (considers, thinks) this thing good—apart from considerations as to what consequences it will have or what purposes it may serve.

To have an unconditional intrinsic preference for one state to its contradictory means, roughly, to *like* it ('as such' or 'in itself'). To have an unconditional intrinsic preference for the absence of a state to its presence means, roughly, to *dislike* or *resent* or *shun* it. To pronounce things good is sometimes to say that we like them, and to pronounce things bad is sometimes to say that we dislike them—and nothing more. But this is only one of a great variety of uses of the words 'good' and 'bad'. Good and bad in the sense of 'liked' and 'disliked' must, for example, be distinguished from good and bad in the sense of 'approved' and 'disapproved'. The first use has an *hedonic*, the second often has a *moral* flavour.

§ 15

Let there be an arbitrary *P*-expression (preference-expression). It is some molecular complex of atomic *P*-expressions.

We shall take it for granted ('axiomatically') that the *P*-expression may be transformed according to the principles of tautological transformations of the Logic of Propositions. For example: If the *P*-expression is a conjunction of atomic *P*-expressions, the order of the conjuncts may be altered without affecting the truth-value of the expression.

We also take it for granted that the expressions to the left and to the right of the sign P in the atomic constituents of the P-expression may be transformed according to the principles of tautological transformations of the Logic of Propositions —*provided that new variables are not introduced in these expressions through the transformation.* For example: If an expression to the left or to the right of the sign P in some atomic constituent is a conjunction of variables, the order of the conjuncts may be altered without affecting the truth-value of the P-expression.

We make a list of all the variables, p, q, r, . . . , which occur in the entire P-expression. They determine the Universe of Discourse of the formula.

We then perform in order the following three operations (transformations) on the P-expression:

a] Consider an arbitrary atomic constituent of the expression. We conjoin to the expression to the left of the sign P the negation of the expression to the right of the sign, and conjoin to the expression to the right of the sign P the negation of the expression to the left of this sign. We call this operation 'conjunction'.

For example: Let the atomic constituent in question be the expression $(p\&q)P{\sim}r$. If we perform on it the operation described, we obtain the expression $(p\&q\&{\sim}{\sim}r)P({\sim}r\&{\sim}(p\&q))$.

We replace all atomic constituents of the given P-expression by new atomic constituents, which are obtained from the original ones by performing on them the operation of conjunction. In all atomic constituents of the P-expression, thus transformed, we then replace the expressions to the left and to the right of the sign P by their perfect disjunctive normal forms in terms of the variables, which occur in these expressions themselves. For example: Having first replaced '$(p\&q)P\sim r$' by '$(p\&q\&\sim\sim r)P(\sim r\&\sim(p\&q))$', we then replace the last expression by

$$`(p\&q\&r)P(\sim p\&q\&\sim r \vee p\&\sim q\&\sim r \vee \sim p\&\sim q\&\sim r)'.$$

b] In the P-expression, which is obtained from the original P-expression after these transformations, we replace the atomic P-expressions with conjunctions of atomic P-expressions in accordance with the rule of conjunctive distributivity of disjunctive preferences. For example: the expression

$$(p\&q\&r)P(\sim p\&q\&\sim r \vee p\&\sim q\&\sim r \vee \sim p\&\sim q\&\sim r)$$

is replaced by the expression

$$[(p\&q\&r)P(p\&\sim q\&\sim r)]\&[(p\&q\&r)P(\sim p\&q\&\sim r)] \&[(p\&q\&r)P(\sim p\&\sim q\&\sim r)].$$

We call this operation 'distribution'.

c] Consider an arbitrary atomic constituent of the P-expression, which is obtained from the original P-expression after all the above transformations. Assume, for the sake of argument, that it contains the variables p and q and r, but that it does not contain the variable s, which also belongs to the Universe of Discourse of the formula. ('s' will then occur in some other of the atomic constituents of the formula.) We replace the atomic constituent by a conjunction of two atomic P-expressions. The first is obtained from the original constituent by conjoining 's' to the expressions to the left and to the right of the sign P in the constituent. The second is obtained from the original constituent by conjuncting '$\sim s$' to the expressions to the left and to the right of the sign P in the constituent. For example: We replace the expression $(p\&q\&r)P(p\&\sim q\&\sim r)$ by

$$[(p\&q\&r\&s)P(p\&\sim q\&\sim r\&s)]\& [(p\&q\&r\&\sim s)P(p\&\sim q\&\sim r\&\sim s)].$$

The operation under consideration will be called 'amplification'.

The operation of amplification is applied to every one of the atomic constituents of the P-expression, until the supply of variables is exhausted, *i.e.* until every one of the atomic constituents of the P-expression contains all the variables which occur in the entire expression.

The reader will have noticed how the three operations of conjunction, distribution, and amplification answer to the three axiomatic principles of the Logic of Preference, which we explained on pp. 27 f., 25 f., and 29 f. respectively.

By a *state-description* within a given Universe of Discourse of (propositional) variables one usually understands a conjunction of all the variables and/or their negations. To n variables there answer 2^n logically different state-descriptions. The state-descriptions may be said to describe the different possible global or total states of a world, which can be described in terms of (the descriptions of) n logically independent elementary states of affairs.

When the operations of conjunction, distribution, and amplification have been performed on a given *P*-expression, the atomic constituents of the transformed expression have a uniform structure. Of this structure it is characteristic that the expressions to the left and to the right of the sign *P* in each atomic constituent are state-descriptions within the Universe of Discourse of the given formula. The atomic constituents of the transformed formula, one could say, describe preferences between total states of a world, which can be described within this Universe of Discourse.

The atomic constituents of the formula, which we get when we apply the three operations to a given formula, will be called the *P-constituents* or *preference-constituents* of the given *P*-expression.

Every *P*-expression expresses a truth-function of (the propositions expressed by) its *P*-constituents. If a *P*-expression expresses the tautology of its *P*-constituents, it will be said to be (express) a *P-tautology* or *preference-tautology*.

Which truth-function of its *P*-constituents a given *P*-expression is can be investigated and decided in a truth-table. The distribution of truth-values over the constituents is, however, subject to two restrictions. These restrictions are imposed by the asymmetrical and transitive nature of the relation of preference (cf. above, p. 21 f.). The restrictions are as follows:

(i) Constituents of the form w_1Pw_2 and w_2Pw_1 cannot both be assigned the value 'true' (in the same distribution of truth-values).

(ii) If the $n-1$ first constituents of a sequence of constituents of the form w_1Pw_2, w_2Pw_3, . . . ,

$w_{n-1}Pw_n$, w_1Pw_n are all assigned the value 'true', then the nth constituent must also be assigned the value 'true'.

The letter w with an index is here being used as a meta-variable, representing an arbitrary state-description within the Universe of Discourse of the P-expression under investigation.

§ 16

The five basic principles of our Logic of Preference which were introduced and explained on pp. 21-33, are 'reflected' in the following five formulae of this logic:

$$(pPq) \to \sim(qPp). \tag{1}$$

$$(pPq)\&(qPr) \to (pPr). \tag{2}$$

$$(pPq) \leftrightarrow (p\&\sim q)P(\sim p\&q). \tag{3}$$

$$\begin{aligned}(p \vee q)P(r \vee s) \leftrightarrow [&(p\&\sim r\&\sim s)P(\sim p\&\sim q\&r) \\ &\&(p\&\sim r\&\sim s)P(\sim p\&\sim q\&s) \\ &\&(q\&\sim r\&\sim s)P(\sim p\&\sim q\&r) \\ &\&(q\&\sim r\&\sim s)P(\sim p\&\sim q\&s)].\end{aligned} \tag{4}$$

$$(pPq) \leftrightarrow [(p\&r)P(q\&r)\&(p\&\sim r)P(q\&\sim r)]. \tag{5}$$

The transformations, described in the last section, can easily be used for showing that the five formulae are (express) P-tautologies. The proofs of the formulae are completely trivial, since the principles which are used for transforming the formulae into molecular compounds of P-constituents and for constructing the truth-tables are the very principles which the formulae themselves may be said to 'reflect'.

§ 17

As a sample tautology of the Logic of Preference we shall study the formula

$$(pP\sim p)\&(\sim qPq)\rightarrow(pPq). \tag{6}$$

The first step, *conjunction*, in the transformation of the formula into a complex of P-constituents gives the formula

$$(pP\sim p)\&(\sim qPq)\rightarrow(p\&\sim q)P(\sim p\&q).$$

The second step, *distribution*, is here vacuous. The third step, *amplification*, gives the formula

$$[(p\&q)P(\sim p\&q)]\&[(p\&\sim q)P(\sim p\&\sim q)]$$
$$\&[(p\&\sim q)P(p\&q)]\&[(\sim p\&\sim q)P(\sim p\&q)]$$
$$\rightarrow[(p\&\sim q)P(\sim p\&q)].$$

The formula has five P-constituents. The first is

	'$(p\&q)P(\sim p\&q)$',
the second is	'$(p\&\sim q)P(\sim p\&\sim q)$',
the third is	'$(p\&\sim q)P(p\&q)$',
the fourth is	'$(\sim p\&\sim q)P(\sim p\&q)$',
and the fifth is	'$(p\&\sim q)P(\sim p\&q)$'.

The asymmetry of preferences does not in this case impose any restriction on the distribution of truth-values over the constituents. Transitivity, however, imposes *one* restriction. This is that, if the second and the fourth constituents are true, then the fifth must be true too.

This single restriction on the distribution of truth-values is enough to warrant that the formula is a tautology. For the formula would be false, if and only if, the first four constituents were all of them true and the fifth false. But if the first four constituents are all of them true, then the second and fourth of them are true too. And if the second and fourth are true, the fifth is true. Thus the sole falsifying combination of truth-values in the five constituents, *viz*. the combination $TTTTF$, does not occur in the truth-table. Hence the formula is a preference-tautology.

Remembering our definitions of 'good' and 'bad' in terms of preference (p. 34), we can read the proved formula as follows: 'A good state of affairs is preferred to a bad state of affairs'. Remembering also that preference is a species of betterness (p. 15), we can read the formula: 'A good state of affairs is better than a bad state of affairs', or simply 'Good is better than bad'.

This is not a very surprising result. But it is a nice example of the kind of logical truths that the Logic of Preference has to establish.

That good is better than bad obviously is a *logical* truth. But it is not a truth of 'ordinary' logic. Someone may wish to say that it is a truth 'by definition'. But what *are* the definitions of 'good', 'bad', and 'better', which would show that good is better than bad? It is not at all obvious how this question should be answered. Therefore the derivation of the result from principles of a Logic of Preference is no 'mere triviality'.

§ 18

a] Let there be an atomic P-expression. We replace the expression to the left or to the right of the sign P

by another expression, which is—according to the laws of the Logic of Propositions—tautologically equivalent with the first and *contains the same variables*. Then the new atomic P-expression will be—according to the laws of the Logic of Preference—tautologically equivalent with the original P-expression. That such is the case was taken for granted ('axiomatically') in the description, which we gave on p. 36, of the transformation of P-expressions.

Thus, *e.g.*, $pP \sim \sim q$ is the same preference as pPq, and $(p\&q)P \sim r$ the same as $(q\&p)P \sim r$.

We could, following the directives given on p. 36 f., *prove* that the expression $(pP \sim \sim q) \leftrightarrow (pPq)$ is a P-tautology. Applying the operation of conjunction to the expression, we first obtain the expression

$$(p\& \sim \sim \sim q)P(\sim \sim q\& \sim p) \leftrightarrow (p\& \sim q)P(q\& \sim p).$$

If we replace the expressions to the left and to the right of the signs P by their perfect disjunctive normal forms in terms of the variables, which occur in these expressions themselves, we obtain the expression $(p\& \sim q)P(\sim p\&q) \leftrightarrow (p\& \sim q)P(\sim p\&q)$. This is a P-tautology.

(Any P-expression which is a tautology according to the laws of the Logic of Propositions is also a tautology according to the laws of the Logic of Preference. This follows from the nature of the truth-tables.)

The above proof of a P-tautology may be said to be 'uninteresting' on the ground that it was taken for granted that an expression to the left or to the right of the sign P may be replaced by its perfect disjunctive normal form. One can hardly take this for granted without also taking it for granted that the expressions to the left and to the right of the sign P may be replaced by *any* tautological transformations of themselves (in terms of the same variables).

b] Consider an atomic P-expression. We replace the expression to the left or to the right of the sign P by another expression, which is—according to the laws of the Logic of Propositions—tautologically equivalent with the first and *contains only variables, which occur in the given P-expression.* Then the new atomic P-expression is—according to the laws of the Logic of Preference—tautologically equivalent with the original P-expression. That such is the case can be (non-trivially) proved on the basis of the principles of this logic.

Consider, *e.g.*, the expression pPq. We replace 'p' by, say, '$p\&q\vee p\&\sim q$' and 'q' by '$p\&q\vee\sim p\&q$'. Then we obtain the expression $(p\&q\vee p\&\sim q)$ $P(p\&q\vee\sim p\&q)$. If we apply the operation of conjunction to it, we get the expression

$$[(p\&q\vee p\&\sim q)\&\sim(p\&q\vee\sim p\&q)]P[(p\&q\vee\sim p\&q)\&\sim(p\&q\vee p\&\sim q)].$$

If in the above instance we replace the expressions to the left and to the right of the sign P by their perfect disjunctive normal forms in terms of the variables, which occur in these expressions themselves, we obtain the expression $(p\&\sim q)P(\sim p\&q)$. As we know, $(pPq)\leftrightarrow(p\&\sim q)P(\sim p\&q)$ is a P-tautology.

c] Consider an atomic P-expression. We replace

the expression to the left or to the right of the sign P by another expression, which is—according to the laws of the Logic of Propositions—tautologically equivalent with the first but *contains variables, which do not occur in the given P-expression*. Then the new atomic P-expression will, in general, *not* be—according to the laws of the Logic of Preference—tautologically equivalent with the original P-expression. This can easily be seen from an example.

Consider, *e.g.*, the expression pPq. We replace 'p' by '$p\&r \vee p\&\sim r$' and 'q' by '$q\&r \vee q\&\sim r$'. We obtain the expression $(p\&r \vee p\&\sim r)P(q\&r \vee q\&\sim r)$. If we apply conjunction to it, we get the expression

$$[(p\&r \vee p\&\sim r)\&\sim(q\&r \vee q\&\sim r)]P[(q\&r \vee q\&\sim r) \&\sim(p\&r \vee p\&\sim r)].$$

If we replace the expressions to the left and to the right of the sign P in the last expression by their perfect disjunctive normal forms in terms of the variables, which occur in those expressions themselves, we obtain the expression

$$(p\&\sim q\&r \vee p\&\sim q\&\sim r)P(\sim p\&q\&r \vee \sim p\&q\&\sim r).$$

If we apply the operation of distribution, we finally obtain the expression

$$[(p\&\sim q\&r)P(\sim p\&q\&r)] \&[(p\&\sim q\&r)P(\sim p\&q\&\sim r)] \&[(p\&\sim q\&\sim r)P(\sim p\&q\&r)] \&[(p\&\sim q\&\sim r)P(\sim p\&q\&\sim r)].$$

This last expression, however, is not tautologically equivalent with the expression pPq—as can be seen if we construct a truth-table. If they were equivalent, then the expression pPq would entail, for example, the expression

$$(p \& \sim q \& r) P (\sim p \& q \& \sim r),$$

which is equivalent with $(p\&r)P(q\&\sim r)$. This means: that p is preferred to q would then entail that $p\&r$ is preferred to $q\&\sim r$. This would be absurd (cf. above, p. 32).

§ 19

The terms 'extensional' and 'intensional' are used in many senses by logicians. *One* way of using the term 'extensional' would be to call a calculus C_1 *extensional* with regard to a calculus C_2, if, and only if, expressions which are provably equivalent in C_2 are intersubstitutable in expressions of C_1.

Accepting this use of 'extensional', we could say that the Logic of Preference is *not* extensional with regard to the Logic of Propositions. For, expressions which are provably equivalent in the Logic of Propositions, are not, without restriction, intersubstitutable in expressions of the Logic of Preference. The restriction is that the substitution must not introduce new variables into the atomic P-expressions, in which the substitution takes place. If new variables are not introduced, substitution may take place. Perhaps one could, for this reason, call the Logic of Preference a *semi-extensional* calculus.

That there should exist this restriction on substitutability is natural, considering that which we (p. 29) have called the 'holistic' nature of preferences. A preference is subject to a *ceteris paribus* clause. And a *ceteris paribus* clause is relative to a Universe of Discourse. If two such clauses contain different state-descriptions, they are different clauses. A preference of one state of affairs to another, subject to the first clause, is not necessarily the same as a preference between those two states, subject to the second clause. We need not deny that the state p is the *same state of affairs* as $p\&r \vee p\&\sim r$ or the state q the same as $q\&r \vee q\&\sim r$. But the preference of p to q under circumstances, which require the presence of r or the absence of r, is not the *same preference* as a preference of p to q under circumstances, which do not require r to be present or to be absent.

Thus the air of paradox, which the semi-extensional nature of the Logic of Preference may at first sight present, disappears when due attention is paid to the 'holistic' nature of preferences.

§ 20

Consider an arbitrary P-expression. We transform it into a molecular compound of P-constituents according to the method described on p. 35 f. Thereupon we transform the molecular complex, thus obtained, into *its* perfect disjunctive normal form (treating the P-constituents as simple sentences). This normal form is a disjunction of conjunctions of P-constituents and/or negations of P-constituents. We shall also call this normal form the (perfect disjunctive) normal form of the original P-expression.

There is a handy way of testing whether the conjunctions in the normal form of a *P*-expression are consistent, using a diagram of points and arrows:

We represent each one of the state-descriptions, which stand to the left and right of the sign *P* in the *P*-constituents, by a point in a plane. Every *unnegated* *P*-constituent in the conjunction we represent by drawing an arrow from the point representing the state-description to the left of the sign *P* in the *P*-constituent to the point representing the state-description to the right of the sign *P* in it. Having thus pictured the unnegated *P*-constituents, we complete the diagram according to the following rule: If there is an arrow from a first point to a second and from this second to a third, there will have to be an arrow also from the first to the third. The diagram, thus completed, pictures a *consistent* conjunction of *P*-constituents and/or negations of *P*-constituents, if, and only if, the following two conditions are satisfied:

(i) There is no pair of points, between which there are arrows in opposite directions. (Asymmetry of preferences.)

(ii) There is no pair of points, which represent the state-descriptions to the left and the right of the sign *P* in some of the *negated* *P*-constituents of the conjunction, and which is such that there is an arrow from the point, representing the state-description to the left, to the point, representing the state-description to the right of the sign *P*.

If *all* the conjunctions in the normal form of a *P*-expression are inconsistent, we can conclude that the negation of the *P*-expression is a *P*-tautology.

We shall use the method described for showing that the formula $(pP\sim p)\&(\sim qPq)\&\sim(pPq)$ is inconsistent.

The transformation of the formula into a molecular compound of P-constituents yields the formula

$$[(p\&q)P(\sim p\&q)]\&[(p\&\sim q)P(\sim p\&\sim q)] \\ \&[(p\&\sim q)P(p\&q)]\&[(\sim p\&\sim q)P(\sim p\&q)] \\ \&\sim[(p\&\sim q)P(\sim p\&q)].$$

This is already in the perfect disjunctive normal form. (It is a one-termed disjunction.)

The diagram below is a picture of the four unnegated P-constituents in the conjunction:

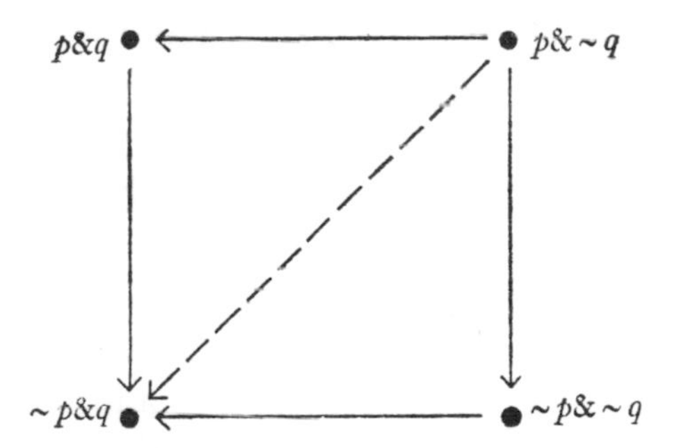

(The dotted arrow enters the picture, when we complete it according to the rule of transitivity.)

The inconsistent (self-contradictory) nature of the formula is shown by the fact that there is an arrow (*viz.* the dotted one) from the point, which represents the state-description to the left of the sign P, to the point, which represents the state-description to the right of the sign P, in the one negated P-constituent (*viz.* '$(p\&\sim q)P(\sim p\&q)$'), of the conjunction.

Since the formula $(pP\sim p)\&(\sim qPq)\&\sim(pPq)$ is thus inconsistent, its negation must be a tautology. Its negation is tautologically equivalent (according to the rules of the Logic of Propositions) to the formula $(pP\sim p)\&(\sim qPq)\rightarrow(pPq)$. This is the formula, which by other methods was already (p. 41 f.) proved to be a P-tautology.

§ 22

We can use diagrams of points and arrows to establish the following (meta-)theorems of the Logic of Preference:

(i) The formula $(pP\sim p)\&(qP\sim q)\&(pPq)$ is consistent. 'Of two good states of affairs, one may be better (worse) than the other.'

(ii) The formula $(\sim pPp)\&(\sim qPq)\&(pPq)$ is consistent. 'Of two bad states of affairs one may be worse (better) than the other.'

The first theorem is proved from this diagram:

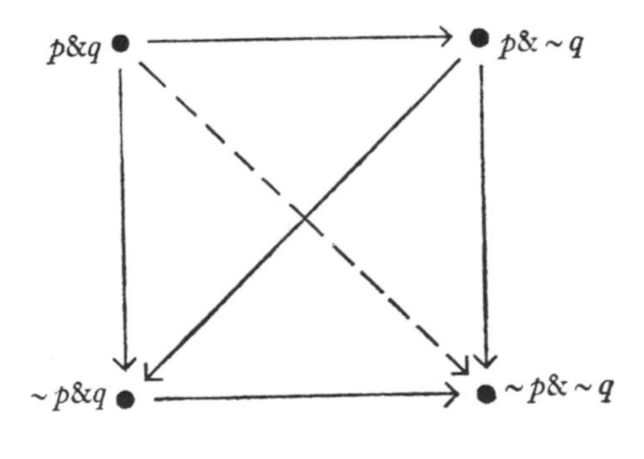

The second theorem is proved from this diagram:

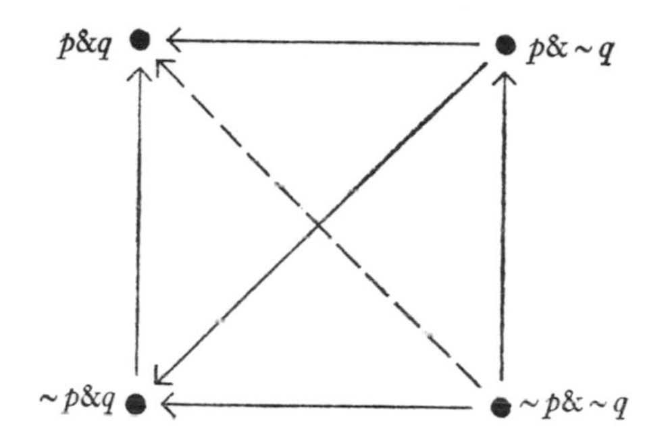

The following diagram is a picture of the fact that the states p and q are both of them good:

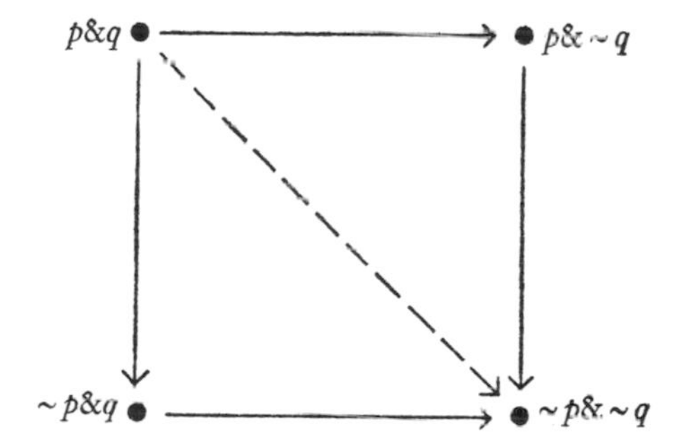

The arrow, which runs diagonally from the point representing the state-description $p \& q$ to the point representing the state-description $\sim p \& \sim q$ must be there, because of the requirement of transitivity. From the diagram we 'read off' the following theorem(s) of our Logic of Preference: 'It is better that both of two good states are present than that only one of them is present or both of them absent.'

§ 23

A state which is neither good nor bad I shall call *indifferent* 'in itself'. The formal definition thus is: 'p is indifferent in itself' = '$\sim(pP\sim p)\&\sim(\sim pPp)$'.

Two states, none of which is preferred to the other, I shall call indifferent 'between themselves'. The definition is: 'p and q are indifferent between themselves' = '$\sim(pPq)\&\sim(qPp)$'.

We could introduce a special symbol I for indifference. The expression pIq shall mean that p and q are indifferent between themselves, and the expression $pI\sim p$ that p is indifferent in itself.

Consider two states, p and q, which are indifferent *in* themselves. Will it necessarily be the case that they are indifferent *between* themselves too? That is: Is $(pI\sim p)\&(qI\sim q)\rightarrow(pIq)$ a P-tautology?

The formula is an abbreviation for the formula

$$[\sim(pP\sim p)\&\sim(\sim pPp)\&\sim(qP\sim q)\&\sim(\sim qPq)] \\ \rightarrow[\sim(pPq)\&\sim(qPp)].$$

If we transform this into a molecular complex of P-constituents, we get the formula

$$\{\sim[(p\&q)P(\sim p\&q)]\&\sim[(p\&\sim q)P(\sim p\&\sim q)] \\ \&\sim[(\sim p\&q)P(p\&q)]\&\sim[(\sim p\&\sim q)P(p\&\sim q)] \\ \&\sim[(p\&q)P(p\&\sim q)]\&\sim[(\sim p\&q)P(\sim p\&\sim q)] \\ \&\sim[(p\&\sim q)P(p\&q)]\&\sim[(\sim p\&\sim q)P(\sim p\&q)]\} \\ \rightarrow\{\sim[(p\&\sim q)P(\sim p\&q)]\&\sim[(\sim p\&q)P(p\&\sim q)]\}.$$

If we reintroduce the abbreviation I, we can also write this last formula in the form

$$\{[(p\&q)I(\sim p\&q)]\&[(p\&\sim q)I(\sim p\&\sim q)]$$
$$\&[(p\&q)I(p\&\sim q)]\&[(\sim p\&q)I(\sim p\&\sim q)]\}$$
$$\to(p\&\sim q)I(\sim p\&q).$$

An investigation of the formula, which is a complex of *P*-constituents, in a truth-table would show that it is *not* a *P*-tautology. The same can more easily be shown by means of an arrow-diagram. Below is a diagram, which illustrates the compatibility of the fact that two states are indifferent in themselves with the possibility that the one is preferred to the other:

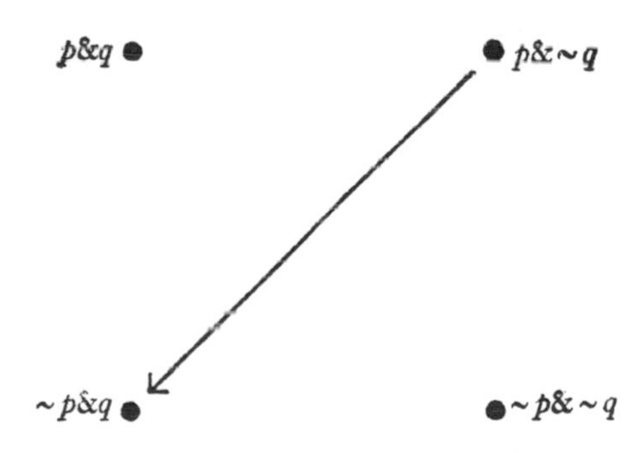

In the diagram there is no arrow either way between the points representing the state-descriptions $p\&q$ and $\sim p\&q$, nor between the points representing the state-descriptions $p\&\sim q$ and $\sim p\&\sim q$. This illustrates that the state p is indifferent in itself. In the diagram, moreover, there is no arrow either way between the points representing the state-descriptions $p\&q$ and $p\&\sim q$, nor between the points representing the state-descriptions $\sim p\&q$ and $\sim p\&\sim q$. This illustrates that the state q is indifferent in itself. There is an arrow from the point representing the state-description $p \& \sim q$ to the point representing the state-description $\sim p \& q$. This illustrates that the state p is preferred to the state q. That these three facts about indifference and preference can be thus illustrated in the same diagram, is a proof of their logical compatibility.

Consider next two states, p and q, which are indifferent between themselves. Assume that p is preferred to a third state r. Will it then necessarily be the case that q too is preferred to r? Is the expression $(pIq)\&(pPr) \rightarrow (qPr)$ a preference-tautology?

Investigation in a truth-table or by means of a diagram would show that the answer is negative. It is, of course, *not* possible for p and q to be indifferent between themselves and p preferred to r and r preferred to q. (For this would go against transitivity and the definition of indifference.) But it *is* possible that p and q are indifferent between themselves and p is preferred to r and yet q not preferred to r, nor r to q. (Then q and r are indifferent between themselves.)

Two states will be said to have *the same value in relation to* a third state, when they are either both preferred to the third state or the third state is preferred to them or all three are indifferent between themselves. The fact that the formula $(pIq)\&(pPr) \rightarrow (qPr)$ is not a tautology may then be said to show that the indifference of two states between themselves does not entail that the two states have the same value relative to any other state.

It may be thought that these findings concerning the notion of indifference are unsatisfactory.

Ought not states, which are indifferent in themselves, to be indifferent between themselves also? And *ought* not states, which are indifferent between themselves, to have the same value relative to all other states? Should we not, therefore, amend our definition of indifference in such a way that the concept satisfies these two conditions?

There is, however, another way of reacting to these findings. Instead of amending our definition of indifference, we can distinguish between *two* notions of indifference. One is a notion of *weak indifference*. This is the notion which we have already defined and for which we introduced the symbol I. The other notion is a notion of *strong indifference*. This notion we have not yet defined. Strong indifference I shall also call (*value-*) *equality*. I shall introduce for it the symbol E.

§ 24

The reason why we ought to distinguish between two concepts of indifference is connected with the 'holistic' nature of preferences.

Consider a Universe of Discourse of three variables p, q, and r. There are eight possible total states of the world, which can be described in the terms of this universe. These are the states described by the eight state-descriptions $p\&q\&r$, . . . , $\sim p\&\sim q\&\sim r$.

The expression pPq means, according to the explanations which we have given, that the state $p\&\sim q$ is *under all circumstances* preferred to the state $\sim p\&q$ (as end-states of contemplated transformations of the world as it is at present). The phrase 'all circumstances' here means 'all conjunctions of states and/or their negations other than p and q themselves'. That the preference holds 'under all circumstances' means that the conjunction of $p\&\sim q$ with any such conjunction of states and/or their negations is preferred to the conjunction of $\sim p\&q$ with *the same* conjunction of states and/or their negations.

If the total state of the world is described in terms of the variables p and q and r, then 'all circumstances' are the states r and $\sim r$. That p is preferred to q then means that the total state $p\&\sim q\&r$ is preferred to the total state $\sim p\&q\&r$ *and* the total state $p\&\sim q\&\sim r$ to the total state $\sim p\&q\&\sim r$.

It follows from the above that the expression $\sim(pPq)$ will mean that, *under some circumstances*, the state $p\&\sim q$ is *not* preferred to the state $\sim p\&q$. (It does not follow that, under some circumstances, the state $\sim p\&q$ *is* preferred to the state $p\&\sim q$.)

For example: If $p\&\sim q\&r$ is preferred to $\sim p\&q\&r$ but $p\&\sim q\&\sim r$ is not preferred to $\sim p\&q\&\sim r$, then p is *not* (unconditionally) preferred to q.

Accordingly, the expression $\sim(pPq)\&\sim(qPp)$ or pIq will mean that, under *some* circumstances, the state $p\&\sim q$ is not preferred to the state $\sim p\&q$ *and*, under *some* circumstances, the state $\sim p\&q$ is not preferred to the state $p\&\sim q$. It should be observed that the two occurrences of 'some' need not refer to the *same* circumstances.

Thus, for example, it may be the case that p and q are indifferent between themselves on the ground that, under circumstances r, p is not preferred to q, but q is preferred to p, and that, under circumstances $\sim r$, q is not preferred to p, but p is preferred to q. The expression

$$\begin{aligned}&\sim[(p\&\sim q\&r)P(\sim p\&q\&r)]\\ &\&[(\sim p\&q\&r)P(p\&\sim q\&r)]\\ &\&\sim[(\sim p\&q\&\sim r)P(p\&\sim q\&\sim r)]\\ &\&[(p\&\sim q\&\sim r)P(\sim p\&q\&\sim r)]\end{aligned}$$

entails the expression $\sim(pPq)\&\sim(qPp)$, *i.e.* pIq.

Indifference, unlike preference, is thus not an attitude 'under all circumstances', but an attitude 'under some circumstances'. Indifference, as defined by us, is not *unconditional* in the same sense as preference, as defined by us, is. So the stronger notion of indifference, of which we are in search, is an 'unconditional indifference' or 'indifference under all circumstances'. This is the notion, which we call (*value-*) *equality*. It is defined as follows:

That the state p is value-equal to the state q shall mean that *under no circumstances* is the state $p\&\sim q$ preferred to the state $\sim p\&q$, or *vice versa.*

If a state and its contradictory state are value-equal, we shall say that the state (and its contradictory) have *zero-value.*

Value-equality is stronger than indifference, *i.e.* states which are value-equal are necessarily indifferent between themselves—but states which are indifferent between themselves are not necessarily value-equal. This immediately follows from the definitions of equality and indifference.

Having zero-value is stronger than being indifferent in itself. This too immediately follows from the definitions.

§ 25

The relation E is *symmetrical*. This can be proved from its definition and the fact that, if we replace the variable p by q and the variable q by p in the expression $\sim(pPq)\&\sim(qPp)$, we get the tautologically equivalent expression $\sim(qPp)\&\sim(pPq)$.

The relation E is also *transitive*. This is 'axiomatic'.

The state p is value-equal with q, if, and only if, the state $p\&\sim q$ is value-equal with $\sim p\&q$. The first equality means, according to our definition, that there are no circumstances under which the state $p\&\sim q$ is preferred to $\sim p\&q$. The second equality again means that there are no circumstances under which the state $p\&\sim q\&\sim(\sim p\&q)$ is preferred to $\sim p\&q\&\sim(p\&\sim q)$. But $p\&\sim q$ is the same state as $p\&\sim q\&\sim(\sim p\&q)$. And $\sim p\&q$ is the same state as $\sim p\&q\&\sim(p\&\sim q)$.

The state pvq is value-equal with r, if, and only if, the state $p\&q\&\sim r$ is value-equal with $\sim p\&\sim q\&r$ *and* the state $p\&\sim q\&\sim r$ with $\sim p\&\sim q\&r$ *and* the state $\sim p\&q\&\sim r$ with $\sim p\&\sim q\&r$. This again is 'axiomatic'. From it and the symmetry of the relation of value-equality there follows a distribution rule for the case when a single state p is value-equal with a disjunction of states qvr.

Let r be a state which is different from p and q and which is not itself a truth-function of other states. Then p is value-equal with q, if, and only if, $p\&r$ is value-equal with $q\&r$ *and* $p\&\sim r$ is value-equal with $q\&\sim r$. This we can prove from the definition of value-equality by means of a *reductio ad absurdum* argument. Assume that, under some circumstances, $p\&r$ would be preferred to $q\&r$, or *vice versa*. Then p would under some circumstances, *viz.* some circumstances which include r, be preferred to q, or *vice versa*. This contradicts the value-equality of p and q. Thus, if p is value-equal with q, then $p\&r$ must be value-equal with $q\&r$. By a similar argument we prove that, if p is value-equal with q, then $p\&\sim r$ must be value-equal with $q\&\sim r$. Assume next that, under some circumstances, p would be preferred to q, or *vice versa*. These circumstances will either include r or they will include $\sim r$. If they do the first, then $p\&r$ cannot be value-equal with $q\&r$. If they do the second, then $p\&\sim r$ cannot be value-equal with $q\&\sim r$. Thus, if $p\&r$ is value-equal with $q\&r$ and $p\&\sim r$ is value-equal with $q\&\sim r$, then p must be value-equal with q.

§ 26

What we mean by an *atomic E*-expression is an expression, which is formed of the sign E with an (atomic or molecular) expression of the Logic of Propositions to its left and to its right. Atomic E-expressions and their molecular compounds will be called E-expressions. The logical study of such expressions might be called the Logic of Value-Equality.

According to what has been said on p. 58 f., the

operations of 'conjunction', 'distribution', and 'amplification', which are valid for P-expressions, are valid for E-expressions too. We can thus transform any given E-expression to a molecular complex of E-constituents by an adaptation of the method, which we described on p. 35 f. The E-constituents of an E-expression state value-equalities between two total states of a world, which can be described in the terms of the Universe of Discourse of the E-expression in question.

Which truth-function of its E-constituents any given E-expression is, can be investigated and decided in a truth-table. The distribution of truth-values over the constituents is subject only to the two restrictions, which are imposed by the symmetrical and transitive nature of the relation of value-equality.

Trivially, these five formulae are E-tautologies (cf. p. 40):

$$(pEq) \rightarrow (qEp). \tag{7}$$

$$(pEq)\&(qEr) \rightarrow (pEr). \tag{8}$$

$$(pEq) \leftrightarrow (p\& \sim q)E(\sim p\&q). \tag{9}$$

$$\begin{aligned}(p\mathrm{v}q)E(r\mathrm{v}s) \leftrightarrow [&(p\& \sim r\& \sim s)E(\sim p\& \sim q\&r)\\ &\&(p\& \sim r\& \sim s)E(\sim p\& \sim q\&s)\\ &\&(q\& \sim r\& \sim s)E(\sim p\& \sim q\&r)\\ &\&(q\& \sim r\& \sim s)E(\sim p\& \sim q\&s)].\end{aligned} \tag{10}$$

$$(pEq) \leftrightarrow [(p\&r)E(q\&r)\&(p\& \sim r)E(q\& \sim r)]. \tag{11}$$

Non-trivially, truth-tables may be used to show that

$$(pE\sim p)\&(qE\sim q)\rightarrow(pEq) \qquad (12)$$

is an E-tautology.

We replace the expression $(pE\sim p)$ by the conjunction of the expressions $(p\&q)E(\sim p\&q)$ and $(p\&\sim q)E(\sim p\&\sim q)$. We replace $(qE\sim q)$ by the conjunction of $(p\&q)E(p\&\sim q)$ and $(\sim p\&q)E(\sim p\&\sim q)$. We replace (pEq) by $(p\&\sim q)E(\sim p\&q)$. The formula (12) has thus become transformed into the following complex of E-constituents:

$$[(p\&q)E(\sim p\&q)\&(p\&\sim q)E(\sim p\&\sim q)$$
$$\&(p\&q)E(p\&\sim q)\&(\sim p\&q)E(\sim p\&\sim q)]$$
$$\rightarrow(p\&\sim q)E(\sim p\&q).$$

It is immediately seen that the restrictions imposed by symmetry and transitivity exclude the combination of truth-values *TTTTF* in the five constituents. In consequence the expression is an E-tautology.

The formula proved can be stated in words as follows: *States of value zero are value-equal.*

§ 27

We can also form 'mixed' molecular compounds of atomic P-expressions and atomic E-expressions. We could call them PE-expressions. Their formal theory we call the Logic of Preference and Value-Equality.

Given any such mixed expression, we can transform it into a molecular compound of constituent expressions in accordance with the rules for transforming P-expressions and E-expressions. Truth-tables can again be used for the purpose of investigating whether a given expression is a tautology or not.

The distribution of truth-values over the P-constituents and the E-constituents of a given PE-expression is subject to the following three restrictions:

(i) Constituents of the form w_1Pw_2 and w_2Pw_1 cannot both be assigned the value 'truc' (in the same distribution of truth-values).

(ii) If the $n-1$ first constituents of a sequence of constituents of the form w_1Pw_2, w_2Pw_3, . . . , $w_{n 1-}Pw_n$, w_1Pw_n are all assigned the value 'true', then the nth constituent must also be assigned the value 'true'.

(iii) If a constituent of the form w_1Ew_2 is assigned the value 'true', then any two PE-constituents, which contain 'w_1' and/or 'w_2' and which are such that the one can be obtained from the other by substituting 'w_1' for 'w_2' and/or 'w_2' for 'w_1', must be assigned *the same* truth-value.

Rule (iii) says in effect that value-equal total states of world have the same value, relative to all other total states of the world. This caters for the restriction upon the distribution of truth-values, which the symmetry and transitivity of the relation E impose.

For example: Let 'w_1Ew_2' and 'w_2Ew_1' be constituents. Each one of them can be obtained from the other by substituting 'w_1' for 'w_2' and 'w_2' for 'w_1'. Therefore, if 'w_1Ew_2' is assigned the value 'true', then 'w_2Ew_1' must be assigned the value 'true' too. Thus the requirement of symmetry is satisfied. Let 'w_1Ew_2' and 'w_2Ew_3' and 'w_1Ew_3' be constituents. The second of them can be obtained from the third by substituting 'w_2' for 'w_1'. The third of them can be obtained from the second by substituting 'w_1' for 'w_2'. Let the first constituent be assigned the value 'true'. Then the second and the third must be assigned the same truth-value. Thus, in particular, if the second is given the value 'true', the third must be given the value 'true' too. This satisfies the requirement of transitivity.

Beside truth-tables, diagrams of points and arrows may also be used for testing whether a given *PE*-expression is a tautology. The expression is first transformed into a complex of constituent parts. This complex of constituents is then transformed into its perfect disjunctive normal form. This is a disjunction of conjunctions of *P*- and *E*-constituents and/or the negations of *P*- and *E*-constituents. The diagrams picture the conjunctions in this normal form.

The rules for constructing the diagrams are as follows:

We represent the state-descriptions, which occur in the *PE*-constituents, by points in a plane.

We illustrate the *unnegated* *P*-constituents of the conjunction in question by drawing an arrow from the point which represents the state-description to the left of the sign *P* in it, to the point which represents the state-description to the right of the sign *P*.

The diagram is now completed in two stages:

First, we consider the pairs of points, which

answer to the state-descriptions in the *unnegated* *E*-constituents of the conjunction. If, in the diagram as it stands, there is an arrow, either way, between one of the points of such a pair and some other point in the diagram, then there must also be a similarly directed arrow between the second point of this pair and that other point in the diagram. If this second arrow is not already in the diagram, it has to be inserted.

Secondly, we ascertain whether there are arrows running from a first point to a second and from this second to a third point, but not from the first to the third point. For all such cases, if any, we complete the diagram by drawing an arrow from the first to the third point.

The diagram, as now completed, is a picture of a *consistent* conjunction of *P*- and *E*-constituents and/or negations of *P*- and *E*-constituents, if, and only if, it satisfies these three requirements:

(i) There are no two points in the diagram, between which there runs an arrow in both directions.

(ii) There is no arrow from a first point to a second point in the diagram such that the first point represents the state-description, which stands to the left, and the second point the state-description, which stands to the right of the sign *P* in some of the *negated* *P*-constituents.

(iii) If a pair of points represents the state-descriptions in some of the *negated* *E*-constituents, then there must exist an arrow either to or from one of the points in the pair to some other point in the diagram, which is not connected by a similarly directed arrow with the second point of the pair. If there exists no such arrow in the diagram, as it stands, the arrow must be inserted and the diagram (if necessary) completed. The diagram must, after the insertion and completion, still satisfy the requirements (i) and (ii).

If all the conjunctions in the normal form of an *EP*-expression are inconsistent, the negation of the *EP*-expression is an *EP*-tautology.

The diagram below shows that

$$(pEq)\&(pPr) \rightarrow (qPr) \qquad (13)$$

is an *EP*-tautology:

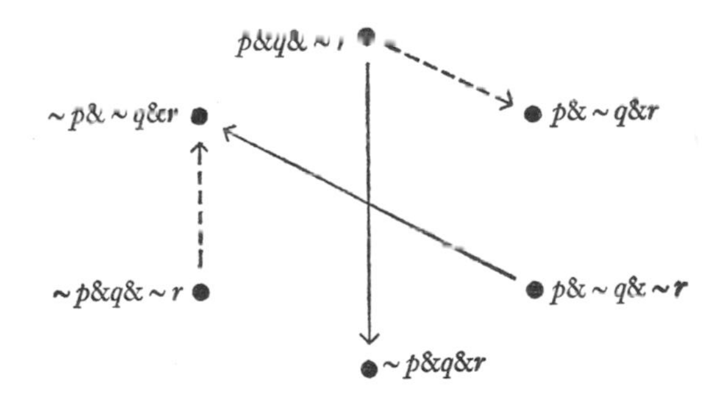

The arrows from the point (which represents the state-description) $p\&q\&\sim r$ to $\sim p\&q\&r$ and from $p\&\sim q\&\sim r$ to $\sim p\&\sim q\&r$ illustrate that the state p is preferred to the state r. The dotted arrow from the point (which represents the state-description) $p\&q\&\sim r$ to $p\&\sim q\&r$ is required by the value-equality of the states $\sim p\&q\&r$ and $p\&\sim q\&r$. The dotted arrow from the point (which represents the state-description) $\sim p\&q\&\sim r$ to $\sim p\&\sim q\&r$ is required by the value-equality of the states $p \& \sim q \& \sim r$ and $\sim p \& q \& \sim r$. These two value-equalities jointly constitute the value-equality of the states p and q. The two dotted arrows again jointly illustrate that the state q is preferred to r. The fact that the two dotted arrows necessarily occur (already) in the picture of the conjunction $(pEq)\&(pPr)$ shows that the conjunction $(pEq)\&(pPr)\& \sim (qPr)$ is inconsistent. Consequently its negation, which is tautologically equivalent to (13), is a tautology.

§ 28

A step in the transformation of a formula into a compound of constituents is the replacement of the formulae to the left and to the right of the signs *P* and *E* by their perfect disjunctive normal forms. This step in the transformation takes place after the operation of 'conjunction' has been performed on the atomic *P*- and/or *E*-expressions in the given formula (cf. above, p. 36).

Assume that the formula to the left or the right of the sign *P* or the sign *E* is self-contradictory (according to the laws of the Logic of Propositions). Then its perfect disjunctive normal form 'vanishes'. It is an *O*-termed disjunction. This is but another way of saying that contradictory formulae have no perfect disjunctive normal form. Special rules must therefore be given for the cases, when self-contradictory expressions stand to the left or to the right of '*P*' or '*E*'.

a] When the expressions both to the left and to the right of the sign *P* are a contradiction, the

P-expression shall be regarded as logically false. Its negation, in other words, is a *P*-tautology. This is not an arbitrary ruling, but a necessary consequence of the asymmetrical and transitive character of the relation of preference. The formula

$$\sim(pPp) \tag{14}$$

must be a *P*-tautology. If we perform the operation of 'conjunction' on it, we obtain '$\sim[(p\&\sim p) P(p\&\sim p)]$'. If we let '*O*' represent a vanishing perfect disjunctive normal form, we may transform the last expression to '$\sim(OPO)$'. '*OPO*' can be treated as a *P*-constituent, which in a truth-table is always assigned the value 'false'. We can then prove that (14) is a *P*-tautology.

b] When the expressions both to the left and to the right of the sign *E* are a contradiction, the *E*-expression shall be regarded as logically true. It is, in other words, an *E*-tautology. This too is not an arbitrary ruling, but a necessary consequence of the symmetrical and transitive character of the relation of (value-) equality. The formula

$$pEp \tag{15}$$

must be an *E*-tautology.

c] For the cases, when the expression to the left but not to the right *or* to the right but not to the left of the signs *P* or *E* is a contradiction, no ruling concerning the necessary truth-value of the formula will be made. Thus, for example, the formulae $(p\&\sim p)Pq$ and $(p\&\sim p)Eq$ are neither provable nor disprovable in our system as it stands.

The cases, when the expression to the left or to the right of the signs *P* or *E* is a tautology, become, after the operation of 'conjunction' has been performed, cases when the expression to the right or to the left of the signs *P* or *E* is a contradiction.